What Great Managers Do Differently

"Unlocking the Secrets of Extraordinary Leadership and Management"

Dr. Ravindran.K.A.
An HR Management Professional, Transformation Coach & Author

First Published in 2024

Copyright © Dr. Ravindran.K.A. 2024

All Rights Reserved.

Title: **"What Great Managers Do Differently"**

ISBN:9798322811220

No part of this book may be reproduced or transmitted in any form whatsoever, electronic or mechanical, including photocopying recording or by any informational storage or retrieval system without the expressed written, dated and signed permission from the author.

LIMITS OF LIABILITY/DISCLAIMER OF WARRANTY: The author of this book has used his best efforts in making this content. The author makes no representation or warranties concerning the accuracy, applicability or completeness of the contents. They disclaim any warranties (expressed or implied) or merchantability for any particular purpose. The author shall in no event be held liable for any loss or other damages, including but not limited to special, incidental, consequential or other damages. The information presented in this publication is compiled from sources believed to be accurate, however, the author assumes no responsibility for errors or omissions. The information in this publication is not intended to replace or substitute professional advice. The strategies outlined in this book may not be suitable for every individual and are not meant to provide individualized advice or recommendations. The advice and strategies found within may not be suitable for every situation. This work is sold with the understanding that the author holds no responsibility for the results accrued from the advice in this book.

All disputes are subject to Delhi jurisdiction only.

"I Dedicate this book to my
Teachers, Mentors and Leaders
who have guided, supported, motivated and encouraged me throughout my journey towards professional Leadership."

Table of Contents

Page No.

Acknowledgement
06

Preface
07

Chapter 1: The Foundations of Great Management
10
- Defining the role of a manager
- Understanding the core responsibilities
- Exploring the qualities of successful managers

Chapter 2: Effective Communication and Active Listening
15
- The power of effective communication
- Developing active listening skills
- Overcoming communication barriers

Chapter 3: Building Trust and Creating a Positive Work Culture
20
- Establishing trust within the team
- Fostering a positive work environment
- Promoting inclusivity and diversity

Chapter 4: Empowering and Developing Employees
26
- Delegating tasks and responsibilities
- Providing opportunities for growth and development
- Coaching and mentoring for success

Chapter 5: Setting Clear Goals and Expectations
32

- The importance of goal setting
- Aligning individual goals with organizational objectives
- Communicating expectations effectively

Chapter 6: Leading by Example and Inspiring Others 37
- Being a role model for the team
- Motivating and inspiring employees
- Encouraging innovation and creativity

Chapter 7: Problem-Solving and Decision-Making 42
- Approaching problem-solving effectively
- Making informed decisions
- Handling crises and conflicts

Chapter 8: Managing Conflict and Nurturing Collaboration 47
- Resolving conflicts within the team
- Promoting collaboration and teamwork
- Building strong relationships

Chapter 9: Recognizing and Rewarding Achievement 53
- Acknowledging and appreciating employee contributions
- Implementing effective recognition programs
- Providing meaningful rewards and incentives

Chapter 10: Continuous Learning and Adaptability 58
- Embracing a growth mindset
- Encouraging a culture of learning
- Adapting to change and uncertainty

Conclusion:
62

Summarizing the key points discussed throughout the book, the conclusion emphasizes the importance of great management practices and the positive impact they can have on teams and organizations. It offers a final call to action for readers to implement these strategies and become exceptional managers themselves.

ACKNOWLEDGEMENT

As I pen down the final words of **"What Great Managers Do Differently,"** I am compelled to express my gratitude to the numerous individuals who have contributed to the creation of this book. This journey has been one of inspiration, learning and collaboration, and I am truly thankful for the support and encouragement I have received.

First and foremost, my heartfelt appreciation goes to the dedicated professionals and industry leaders whose stories and experiences enrich the pages of this book. Your insights have added depth and authenticity, serving as invaluable lessons for aspiring and seasoned managers alike.

I am indebted to my colleagues and mentors who have provided guidance, constructive feedback and unwavering support. Your collective wisdom has been instrumental in shaping the ideas presented in this book.

To my family, whose understanding, patience and encouragement have sustained me through the highs and lows of this endeavour, I offer my deepest thanks. Your belief in the importance of effective management and the positive impact it can have on individuals and organizations has been a constant source of inspiration.

Finally, to the readers who embark on this journey, I extend my sincere appreciation. Your curiosity and commitment to personal and professional growth are the driving forces behind the creation of this book. I hope the insights and strategies shared within these pages prove valuable in your quest to become exceptional managers.

With gratitude,

Dr. Ravindran.K.A.
An HR Management Professional, Transformation Coach & Author

PREFACE

What Great Managers do Differently

Welcome to the preface of the book titled **"What Great Managers Do Differently"** In these pages, we embark on a journey to explore the qualities, skills and practices that distinguish exceptional managers from the rest. Whether you are an aspiring manager, a seasoned leader or simply interested in understanding the art of effective management, this book aims to provide valuable insights and practical strategies to help you excel in your role.

The role of a manager has evolved significantly over the years. It is no longer solely about supervising tasks or overseeing operations. Great managers understand that their primary responsibility is to lead and inspire their teams towards success. They possess a unique set of qualities and practices that allow them to foster a positive work culture, empower their employees, and drive exceptional performance.

This book is born out of a deep belief in the power of effective management and the profound impact it can have on individuals, teams and organizations. Drawing on research, real-life experiences and examples from Indian industry leaders, I have crafted a comprehensive guide that explores the multifaceted nature of great management.

Each chapter explores a specific aspect of what great managers do differently. From the foundations of great management to effective communication, building trust, empowering employees, setting clear goals, leading by example, problem-solving, nurturing collaboration, recognizing achievement, and embracing continuous learning, I cover a wide range of topics essential for successful management.

Throughout this book, we emphasize the importance of people-centered leadership. Great managers understand that their success lies in the success of their team members. They prioritize open communication, active listening and building strong relationships based on trust and respect. They inspire their teams, foster collaboration and create an environment where individuals can thrive and reach their full potential.

Moreover, this book recognizes the rich tapestry of Indian industry leaders who have made significant contributions to the field of management. We draw on their experiences, stories and best practices to provide relevant examples that resonate with readers in an Indian context. By showcasing these exceptional leaders, we aim to inspire and motivate managers to adapt their strategies and learn from their successes and challenges.

It is important to note that effective management is not a one-size-fits-all approach. Each manager brings their unique personality, experiences and perspectives to the role. However, there are common principles and strategies that can be applied universally. This book aims to provide a framework that managers can adapt and customize to suit their specific circumstances and the needs of their teams.

I invite you to embark on this journey of discovery and growth. Whether you are a new manager looking to establish a strong foundation, a seasoned leader seeking fresh insights, or an individual interested in understanding the qualities of great managers, this book offers a wealth of knowledge and practical guidance.

As you immerse yourself in the chapters that follow, we encourage you to reflect on your own management style and consider how you can incorporate the principles and strategies presented into your everyday practice. Embrace the challenges, seize the opportunities and foster an environment where greatness can flourish.

I strongly believe this book will empower you to become a great manager who not only achieves outstanding results but also positively impacts the lives of your team members. By leading with integrity, compassion and a genuine commitment to their growth and success, you can create a lasting legacy that extends far beyond the workplace.

Thank you for joining me on this journey. May this book serve as a source of inspiration, practical insights and encouragement as you strive to become a truly exceptional manager who makes a difference.

Best wishes on your path to becoming a great manager.

Dr. Ravindran.K.A.

An HR Management Professional, Transformation Coach & Author

*"Leadership is not about being in charge.
It is about taking care of those in your charge."*

- Ratan Tata

Chapter 1
The Foundations of Great Management

Introduction:

In this chapter, we lay the groundwork for understanding the foundations of great management. We delve into the role of a manager, their core responsibilities and the qualities that set successful managers apart. By exploring these key aspects, we gain insights into what it takes to excel in a managerial role.

Defining the role of a manager:

A manager plays a pivotal role in an organization, responsible for overseeing teams, driving productivity and achieving business goals. They act as a connecting bridge between top management and employees, ensuring effective communication and implementation of strategies. A manager's role encompasses various functions, including planning, organizing, coordinating and controlling activities within their team or department.

Understanding the core responsibilities:

1. *Goal-setting and Planning*: Great Managers are skillful at setting clear and measurable goals aligned with the organization's objectives. They develop strategic plans and action steps to achieve those goals while considering available resources and potential challenges.

2. *Organizing and Resource Management*: Managers organize and allocate resources efficiently to optimize productivity and achieve desired outcomes. This includes assigning tasks, managing workloads and ensuring the availability of necessary tools and resources.

3. *Team Building and Leadership*: Successful managers build strong teams by attracting, developing and retaining top talents. They foster a positive work culture, inspire team members and lead by example. Effective leadership involves providing

guidance, coaching and support to help individuals reach their full potential.

4. *Communication and Collaboration*: Managers must possess excellent communication skills to convey expectations, provide feedback and facilitate collaboration among team members. They ensure a free flow of information and actively listen to their team and encourage open discussions.

Exploring the qualities of successful managers:

1. *Integrity and Ethics*: Great managers uphold high ethical standards and demonstrate integrity in their actions. They lead with honesty, transparency and fairness, earning the trust and respect of their team.

2. *Emotional Intelligence*: Successful managers possess emotional intelligence, which enables them to understand and manage their own emotions while empathizing with others. This skill enhances to build strong relationships, resolve conflicts and foster a positive work environment.

3. *Adaptability and Resilience*: Managers need to be adaptable in the face of change and resilient when encountering obstacles. They embrace innovation, proactively seek solutions and navigate challenges with a positive mindset.

4. *Decision-Making and Problem-Solving*: Effective managers are skilled decision-makers who can analyze situations, weigh alternatives, and make informed choices. They are also proficient problem solvers, identifying root causes and implementing solutions to address issues.

Let us understand the qualities and behaviours exhibited by Great Industry Leaders that have contributed to their success. In each chapter, I will be sharing the success story of a few Great Leaders who have made significant contributions to the field of management and their relevant industry/organisation.

- Success Story: Ratan Tata

Ratan Tata, the former chairman of Tata Group, is renowned for his visionary leadership. He emphasized the importance of integrity, ethics and long-term strategy in his business. His commitment to social responsibility and sustainable practices showcased his dedication to building a strong foundation for the Tata brand.

Summary of Learnings:

- Managers play a crucial role in organisations, bridging the gap between top management and employees.

- Their core responsibilities include goal-setting, organizing, team building and communication.

- Successful managers exhibit qualities such as integrity, emotional intelligence, adaptability and decision-making prowess.

"I believe that leadership isn't about being the boss, it's about taking care of the people who work for you"

— *Indra Nooyi*

Chapter 2
Effective Communication and Active Listening

Introduction:

In this chapter, we delve into the crucial skills of effective communication and active listening that set great managers apart. We explore the power of effective communication, the importance of developing active listening skills, and strategies for overcoming common communication barriers. By mastering these skills, managers can foster understanding, build strong relationships and enhance overall team performance.

The Power of Effective Communication:

Effective communication is the cornerstone of successful management. It involves the clear and concise exchange of information, ideas and expectations to achieve shared understanding. When managers communicate effectively, they can inspire, motivate, and align their teams towards common goals. The power of effective communication lies in its ability to build trust, resolve conflicts and create a positive work environment.

Developing Active Listening Skills:

Active listening is a vital component of effective communication. It involves fully focusing on the speaker, understanding their message and providing appropriate feedback. Great managers understand that listening attentively demonstrates respect, empathy and a genuine interest in their team members' perspectives. By developing active listening skills, managers can enhance collaboration, gain valuable insights and nurture stronger relationships.

Strategies for Overcoming Communication Barriers:

Despite the importance of effective communication, various barriers can hinder the process. Great managers are proactive in identifying and overcoming these barriers. Here are some strategies to overcome common communication challenges:

1. *Clear and Concise Communication*: Managers should strive for clarity in their communication, avoiding jargon or ambiguous language. By using simple and straightforward language, they ensure that their message or intent is easily understood by everyone.

2. *Active and Engaged Listening*: Actively listening to team members involves maintaining eye contact, nodding and providing verbal and nonverbal cues to show understanding and interest. Managers should refrain from interrupting and allow the speaker to express themselves fully.

3. *Feedback and Confirmation*: To ensure understanding, managers should provide feedback by paraphrasing or summarizing what they have heard. This not only confirms comprehension but also allows the speaker to clarify any misunderstandings.

4. *Creating a Safe and Open Environment*: Managers should cultivate an environment where team members feel comfortable expressing their thoughts and concerns openly. Encouraging a culture of open communication and valuing diverse perspectives can help overcome communication barriers.

5. *Utilizing Various Communication Channels*: Different individuals have different communication preferences. Managers should leverage various communication channels, such as face-to-face conversations, emails or team meetings, to cater to the needs and preferences of their team members.

Effective communication and active listening are crucial skills for managers to ensure clear understanding and foster productive relationships within their teams and across the organisation.

Success Story: Indra Nooyi

Indra Nooyi, the former CEO of PepsiCo, was known for her exceptional communication skills. She believed in open and transparent communication, actively listening to her employees' concerns and encouraging diverse perspectives. Her ability to effectively communicate the company's vision and values contributed to PepsiCo's success.

Summary of Learnings:

- Effective communication is essential for successful management, as it builds trust and fosters a positive work environment.

- Active listening demonstrates respect, empathy and understanding, leading to stronger relationships and hence improved collaboration.

- Overcoming communication barriers requires clear and concise communication, active listening, providing feedback, creating a safe environment and utilizing various communication channels.

"The future of any corporation is as good as the value system of the leaders and followers in the organization."

- N. R. Narayana Murthy

Chapter 3
Building Trust and Creating a Positive Work Culture

Introduction:

In this chapter, we explore the importance of building trust and creating a positive work culture in effective management. We delve into strategies for establishing trust within the team, fostering a positive work environment and promoting inclusivity and diversity. By prioritizing these aspects, managers can cultivate a supportive atmosphere where employees feel valued, engaged and motivated to perform at their best.

Establishing Trust Within the Team:

Trust is the foundation of any successful team. Managers play a crucial role in establishing and nurturing trust among team members. Here are key strategies to build trust:

1. *Lead by Example:* Managers should exhibit trustworthiness in their actions, follow through on commitments and demonstrate integrity. When team members witness their manager's trustworthiness, it sets a positive example for the entire team.

2. *Open and Transparent Communication*: Encouraging open and transparent communication fosters trust. Managers should share relevant information, provide regular updates and be receptive to feedback and concerns. This transparency builds trust by creating an environment of honesty and accountability.

3. *Empowerment and Autonomy*: Trust is nurtured when managers empower their team members and provide them with autonomy in decision-making. Allowing employees to take ownership of their work and offering support when needed shows trust in their abilities and fosters a sense of ownership and accountability.

Fostering a Positive Work Environment:

A positive work environment is crucial for productivity, collaboration and employee satisfaction. Great managers prioritize creating a positive work culture using the following strategies:

1. *Recognition and Appreciation*: Managers should recognize and appreciate the efforts and achievements of their team members. Acknowledging individual and team contributions fosters a positive atmosphere, boosts morale and encourages continued excellence. This kind of acknowledgement and recognition should be cascaded across the team/organisation.

2. *Support and Development*: Managers should support and provide opportunities for professional development for their team members. By investing in their employees' growth and well-being, managers create a positive environment that values individuals' success and continuous improvement.

3. *Work-Life Balance*: Promoting work-life balance demonstrates concern for employee well-being and helps reduce burnout. Managers should encourage healthy work-life integration by providing flexibility, promoting self-care and discouraging overwork.

Promoting Inclusivity and Diversity:

Inclusive and diverse work environments benefit both individuals and organizations. Great managers foster inclusivity and diversity by implementing the following strategies:

1. *Embrace Different Perspectives*: Managers should value and encourage diverse perspectives within their teams. By creating an environment where various ideas are welcomed and respected, managers can harness the power of diverse thinking and innovation.

2. *Eliminate Bias and Discrimination*: Managers should ensure fair and unbiased treatment of all employees, promoting equal opportunities and addressing any discriminatory behaviour promptly. They should establish policies and practices that foster an inclusive and respectful workplace.

3. *Employee Resource Groups and Training*: Managers can support inclusivity and diversity by establishing employee resource groups and providing training on unconscious bias, cultural sensitivity and diversity awareness. These initiatives help create a sense of belonging and promote understanding among team members.

Building trust and creating a positive work culture is essential for fostering collaboration, employee engagement and productivity.

- Success Story: N. R. Narayana Murthy

N. R. Narayana Murthy, co-founder of Infosys, emphasized the importance of building trust with his employees. By promoting a transparent and inclusive work culture, he created an environment where employees felt valued and empowered to contribute their best. Murthy's commitment to integrity and fairness played a vital role in Infosys' growth and success.

Summary of Learnings:

- Building trust and respecting each other is essential for effective teamwork and collaboration.

- Fostering a positive work environment boosts morale, productivity and employee satisfaction which leads to high retention of employees and helps to reduce attrition and its cost.

- Promoting inclusivity and diversity fosters innovation, creativity and a sense of belonging within the organisation.

"Leadership is about having the confidence to change the world"

- *Kiran Mazumdar-Shaw*

Chapter 4
Empowering and Developing Employees

Introduction:

In this chapter, we explore the significance of empowering and developing employees as a crucial aspect of effective management. We delve into strategies for delegating tasks and responsibilities, providing opportunities for growth and development and fostering a culture of coaching and mentoring. By prioritizing these practices, managers can unlock their team's full potential, enhance individual skills and contribute to the overall success of the organization.

Delegating Tasks and Responsibilities:

Delegation is a vital skill for managers, enabling them to distribute tasks and responsibilities effectively among team members. Here are key strategies for successful delegation:

1. *Assessing Strengths and Capabilities*: Managers should have a clear understanding of their team members' strengths, skills and areas for development. By aligning tasks with individuals' strengths, managers can maximize the team's productivity and job satisfaction.

2. *Providing Clear Instructions and Expectations*: Effective delegation requires managers to provide clear instructions, guidelines and expectations for the assigned tasks. Clear communication ensures that team members understand their roles, responsibilities and desired outcomes.

3. *Granting Autonomy and Accountability*: Delegation involves empowering employees with the necessary authority and autonomy to complete their tasks. Managers should trust their team members, allow them to make decisions within their scope, and hold them accountable for their work.

Providing Opportunities for Growth and Development:

Investing in the growth and development of employees is essential for their long-term success and the organization's overall progress. Here are strategies for providing growth opportunities:

1. *Training and Skill Development*: Managers should identify skills gaps within their team and provide relevant training opportunities. This could include workshops, seminars, online courses or on-the-job training to enhance knowledge and capabilities.

2. *Challenging Assignments and Stretch Goals*: Offering challenging assignments that push employees out of their comfort zones fosters growth. Managers should provide opportunities for team members to take on new responsibilities and tackle projects that develop their skills and expand their capabilities.

3. *Encouraging Learning and Knowledge Sharing*: Promoting a culture of continuous learning within the team cultivates a growth mindset. Managers can encourage employees to share their expertise and experiences, fostering a collaborative environment where learning is valued.

Coaching and Mentoring for Success:

Coaching and mentoring are powerful tools for supporting employee growth, enhancing performance and fostering professional development. Here are strategies for effective coaching and mentoring:

1. *Establishing Regular Feedback Sessions*: Managers should conduct regular one-on-one meetings to provide feedback, guidance and support to their team members. These sessions offer an opportunity to discuss goals, challenges and areas for improvement.

2. *Providing Constructive Feedback*: Managers should offer specific, constructive feedback that focuses on strengths and areas for growth. They should highlight accomplishments, address challenges and provide actionable suggestions for improvement.

3. *Acting as a Role Model and Mentor*: Managers should lead by example and serve as mentors, offering guidance, sharing experiences and providing career advice. They can support employees' professional growth by fostering a mentorship culture within the organization.

- Success Story: Kiran Mazumdar-Shaw

Kiran Mazumdar-Shaw, the founder of Biocon Limited, prioritized employee empowerment and development. She established a culture of continuous learning, providing her employees with opportunities to upskill and take on challenging projects. Mazumdar-Shaw's focus on nurturing talent and fostering innovation propelled Biocon to become a global biopharmaceutical company.

Summary of Learnings:

- Delegating tasks and responsibilities effectively enhances productivity and job satisfaction.

- Providing growth opportunities supports employees' long-term success and contributes to organizational progress.

- Coaching and mentoring empower employees, enhance performance and foster professional development.

> "The best Leaders don't focus on their own success, but on the success of their team"
>
> - Sundar Pichai

Chapter 5
Setting Clear Goals and Expectations

Introduction:

In this chapter, we explore the significance of setting clear goals and expectations in effective management. We delve into the importance of goal setting, aligning individual goals with organizational objectives and communicating expectations effectively. By mastering these practices, managers can drive performance, enhance focus and foster a sense of purpose within their teams.

The Importance of Goal Setting:

Goal setting is a crucial aspect of effective management as it provides direction, focus and motivation for individuals as well as the entire teams. Here are key points highlighting the importance of goal setting:

1. *Clarity and Direction*: Clear goals provide a sense of direction and purpose, guiding employees towards desired outcomes. They help prioritize tasks, make informed decisions and focus efforts on achieving specific results.

2. *Motivation and Engagement*: Goals that are challenging; yet attainable, motivate individuals to push their limits, enhance performance and feel a sense of accomplishment. Well-defined goals foster employee engagement, as they understand the purpose behind their work.

3. *Measurement and Evaluation*: Goals provide a basis for periodical measurement and evaluation of progress. By setting clear benchmarks and milestones, managers can assess performance, provide performance feedback and make necessary adjustments to ensure continuous improvement.

Aligning Individual Goals with Organizational Objectives:

To achieve overall organizational success, individual goals must align with broader objectives. Here are strategies for aligning individual and organizational goals:

1. *Cascading Goals*: Managers should ensure that individual goals align with departmental and organizational objectives. By cascading goals from top to bottom, managers create a cohesive framework where everyone's efforts contribute to the larger picture.

2. *Collaborative Goal-Setting*: Involving employees in the goal-setting process fosters ownership and commitment. Managers should engage team members in meaningful discussions, solicit their input and align individual goals with their skills, interests and aspirations.

3. *Regular Progress Review*: Managers should conduct regular progress reviews to assess how individual goals align with organizational objectives. These reviews allow for adjustments, realignment and necessary support to ensure alignment remains intact.

Communicating Expectations Effectively:

Effective communication of expectations is vital for clarity, accountability and performance. Here are strategies for communicating expectations effectively:

1. *Clear and Specific Communication*: Managers should articulate expectations clearly, leaving no room for ambiguity. They should provide specific details regarding deliverables, timelines, quality standards and any other relevant parameters.

2. *Active Listening and Feedback*: Managers should actively listen to employees' perspectives, concerns and questions to ensure mutual understanding. Providing regular feedback helps

employees understand where they stand and make necessary adjustments to meet expectations.

3. *Ongoing Communication*: Managers should foster open channels of communication, encouraging employees to seek clarifications or discuss challenges. Regular check-ins and updates ensure that expectations are understood and potential issues are addressed promptly.

Setting clear goals and expectations helps align individual efforts with organizational objectives, enabling teams to work cohesively towards shared targets.

- Success Story: Sundar Pichai

Sundar Pichai, the CEO of Google and Alphabet Inc., is known for his ability to set ambitious yet attainable goals. He encourages his teams to think big and provides a clear vision for the company's future. Pichai's goal-setting approach has played a significant role in Google's innovation and success.

Summary of Learnings:

- Goal setting provides clarity, motivation and direction for individuals and teams.

- Aligning individual goals with organizational objectives ensures collective progress and success.

- Effective communication of expectations fosters clarity, accountability and performance outcomes.

"Success is not about the destination, it's the process"

- Mary Kom

Chapter 6
Leading by Example and Inspiring Others

Introduction:

In this chapter, we explore the importance of leading by example and inspiring others in effective management. We delve into the role of being a role model for the team, strategies for motivating and inspiring employees and fostering a culture of innovation and creativity. By mastering these practices, managers can create a positive work environment, foster employee engagement and drive organizational success.

Being a Role Model for the Team:

As a manager, being a role model is essential in setting the tone for the team and establishing a positive work culture. Here are key points highlighting the significance of being a role model:

1. *Integrity and Ethics*: Managers should lead with integrity; demonstrating honesty, transparency and ethical behaviour. By upholding high standards of conduct, managers set an example for their team members to follow.

2. *Professionalism and Accountability*: Leading by example involves displaying professionalism, taking responsibility for one's actions and being accountable for results. When managers demonstrate these traits, it inspires employees to do the same.

3. *Continuous Learning and Growth*: Managers should demonstrate a growth mindset, actively seeking opportunities for personal and professional development. By demonstrating a commitment to learning, managers encourage their team members to embrace continuous learning and self-improvement.

Motivating and Inspiring Employees:

Motivation and inspiration are key to fostering a high-performing and engaged team. Here are strategies for motivating and inspiring employees:

1. *Recognition and Appreciation*: Managers should recognize and appreciate the efforts and achievements of their team members. Celebrating successes, providing positive feedback and acknowledging individual contributions boosts morale and motivates employees to excel.

2. *Empowerment and Trust*: Managers should empower their team members by delegating responsibilities, providing autonomy and trusting their abilities. When employees feel trusted and empowered, they are motivated to take ownership of their work and contribute to the organization's success.

3. *Clear Communication and Vision*: Managers should effectively communicate the organization's vision, goals and strategies. By providing a clear sense of purpose and direction, managers inspire employees to align their efforts with the broader objectives, fostering motivation and commitment.

Encouraging Innovation and Creativity:

A culture of innovation and creativity drives organizational growth and success. Here are strategies for fostering innovation and creativity within the team:

1. *Openness to New Ideas*: Managers should encourage employees to share their ideas and perspectives, creating an environment where new ideas are welcomed and valued. By actively seeking input, managers inspire creativity and innovation.

2. *Embracing Risk-Taking*: Managers should create a safe space for employees to take risks and explore new possibilities. Encouraging calculated risk-taking fosters innovation, as employees are empowered to think outside the box and experiment with new approaches.

3. *Providing Resources and Support*: Managers should provide the necessary resources, tools and support to fuel innovation and creativity. This includes allocating time for brainstorming,

offering training or mentorship and creating cross-functional collaboration opportunities.

Great managers lead by example, serving as role models for their teams and inspiring them to reach their full potential.

- Success Story: Mary Kom

Mary Kom, an Olympic bronze medalist and multiple-time world champion boxer, exemplifies the qualities of a great leader. Her determination, discipline and perseverance have inspired countless individuals to pursue their dreams and overcome challenges. Kom's leadership through her sporting achievements demonstrates the power of leading by example.

Summary of Learnings:

- Being a role model sets the tone for the team and establishes a positive work culture.

- Motivating and inspiring employees boosts engagement and performance and enhances job satisfaction.

- Fostering a culture of innovation and creativity drives organizational growth and success.

"Success can only come from raising your own standards, pushing yourself to higher levels, and never stop testing and learning."

- *Mukesh Ambani*

Chapter 7
Problem-Solving and Decision-Making

Introduction:

In this chapter, we delve into the essential skills of problem-solving and decision-making as effective management. We explore strategies for approaching problem-solving effectively, making informed decisions and handling crises and conflicts. By mastering these practices; managers can navigate challenges, drive innovation and maintain a positive work environment.

Approaching Problem-Solving Effectively:

Problem-solving is a critical skill for managers as they encounter various challenges in their roles. Here are key points highlighting effective problem-solving strategies:

1. *Define the Problem*: Managers should clearly define the problem at hand, ensuring a thorough understanding of its scope, impact and underlying causes. This step lays the foundation for finding appropriate solutions.

2. *Gather Information*: Gathering relevant information is crucial in problem-solving. Managers should conduct research, seek input from team members or experts, and collect data to gain insights and informed decision-making.

3. *Analyze and Evaluate Options*: Managers should analyze potential solutions, evaluating their feasibility, effectiveness and potential risks. This analysis helps identify the most viable course of action.

Making Informed Decisions:

Effective decision-making is vital for managers to drive progress and achieve desired outcomes. Here are strategies for making informed decisions:

1. *Define Decision Criteria*: Managers should establish clear criteria that align with organizational goals and values. These

criteria serve as benchmarks for evaluating options and making decisions based on relevant factors.

2. *Assess Risks and Benefits*: Managers should consider the risks and benefits associated with each option. A thorough analysis helps weigh potential outcomes and make informed decisions that maximize benefits while mitigating risks.

3. *Seek Input and Collaboration*: Involving team members and stakeholders in the decision-making process fosters collaboration and ensures diverse perspectives are considered. This collaborative approach leads to better decisions and increased buy-in from those affected by the outcomes.

Handling Crises and Conflicts:

Managers often face crises and conflicts that require prompt and effective resolution. Here are strategies for handling crises and conflicts:

1. *Stay Calm and Objective*: Managers should maintain calm and approach crises or conflicts with a level-headed mindset. By staying calm, they can analyze the situation objectively and make rational decisions.

2. *Communicate Clearly*: Effective communication is crucial during crises and conflicts. Managers should communicate with transparency, clarity and empathy to address concerns, diffuse tension and provide guidance.

3. *Mediation and Conflict Resolution*: Managers should employ mediation techniques to facilitate constructive dialogue and resolution of conflicts. They should encourage open communication, active listening and seek win-win solutions whenever possible.

Managers face various challenges that require effective problem-solving skills and sound decision-making abilities.

- Success Story: Mukesh Ambani

Mukesh Ambani, the Chairman and Managing Director of Reliance Industries, has demonstrated exceptional problem-solving skills throughout his career. He led Reliance's successful transformation from a petrochemical company to a global conglomerate, making strategic decisions that propelled the company's growth. Ambani's ability to navigate complex challenges showcases the importance of decisive problem-solving.

Summary of Learnings:

- Effective problem-solving involves defining the problem, gathering information and evaluating options.

- Informed decision-making requires clear criteria, risk assessment and collaboration.

- Handling crises and conflicts necessitates staying calm, communicating effectively, and facilitating resolution.

"Leadership is not about how many people you can order around. It's about empowering people to do their best work, so they can assemble in their own communities to take on the world, to dominate their sport, interchange their families and create their own businesses."

- *Adi Godrej*

Chapter 8
Managing Conflict and Nurturing Collaboration

Introduction:

In this chapter, we explore the critical skills of managing conflict and nurturing collaboration in effective management. We delve into strategies for resolving conflicts within the team, promoting collaboration and teamwork, and building strong relationships. By mastering these practices, managers can create a harmonious work environment, enhance team performance and foster a culture of collaboration and trust.

Resolving Conflicts Within the Team:

Conflicts are an inevitable part of team dynamics; effective managers must address them promptly and constructively. Here are key strategies for resolving conflicts within the team:

1. *Identify the Underlying Issues*: Managers should strive to understand the root causes of conflicts by actively listening to all parties involved. By identifying the underlying issues, managers can develop effective solutions that address the core concerns and prevent conflicts from escalating.

2. *Encourage Open Communication*: Creating an environment that encourages open and honest communication is vital for conflict resolution. Managers should foster an atmosphere where team members feel comfortable expressing their perspectives, concerns and feelings. Active listening, empathy and respect play a significant role in resolving conflicts.

3. *Facilitate Mediation and Negotiation*: Managers can act as mediators, facilitating open and constructive dialogue between conflicting parties. By promoting understanding and encouraging compromise, managers can guide the team towards finding mutually agreeable solutions.

Promoting Collaboration and Teamwork:

Collaboration and teamwork are essential for achieving shared goals and driving collective success. Here are strategies for promoting collaboration and teamwork:

1. *Establish a Shared Vision and Goals*: Managers should ensure that the team understands and aligns with the organization's vision and goals. A shared purpose provides a common focus and fosters collaboration towards a unified objective. Clear communication of goals and expectations helps align individual efforts with team goals.

2. *Foster Trust and Psychological Safety*: Trust is the foundation of collaboration. Managers should create an environment where trust and psychological safety are prioritized. Team members should feel comfortable sharing ideas, taking risks and being vulnerable without fear of judgment or negative consequences. Trust-building activities, open communication and transparency contribute to a culture of psychological safety.

3. *Encourage Cross-Functional Collaboration*: Managers should encourage and facilitate collaboration across different departments or areas of expertise. By practicing diverse perspectives, skills and experiences, managers can stimulate creativity, promote innovation and solve complex problems more effectively. Cross-functional collaboration also enhances knowledge sharing and creates a sense of unity within the organization.

Building Strong Relationships:

Strong relationships within the team contribute to a positive work environment and enhanced collaboration. Here are strategies for building strong relationships:

1. *Lead by Example*: Managers should demonstrate respect, empathy and professionalism in their interactions with team members. Modelling positive behaviour establishes a foundation

of trust and builds strong relationships. Managers should also promote a culture of respect and encourage team members to treat each other with dignity and kindness.

2. *Foster a Supportive Culture*: Managers should foster a supportive and inclusive culture within the team. Celebrating successes, providing constructive feedback and recognizing individual contributions help to establish a supportive and nurturing environment. Managers should encourage teamwork, cooperation and a spirit of helping one another.

3. *Foster Team-Building Activities*: Managers can organize team-building activities that promote bonding, trust and camaraderie. These activities can include collaborative projects, team outings, workshops or social events. Team-building activities create opportunities for team members to get to know each other better, develop mutual understanding and strengthen relationships.

- Success Story: Adi Godrej

Adi Godrej, the chairman of the Godrej Group, has emphasized the significance of collaboration within his organization. By promoting cross-functional collaboration and encouraging open dialogue, he fostered a culture of teamwork and unity. Godrej's efforts to manage conflicts constructively have contributed to the sustained success of the Godrej Group.

Summary of Learnings:

- Resolving conflicts requires identifying underlying issues, promoting open communication and facilitating mediation and negotiation.

- Promoting collaboration involves establishing a shared vision, fostering trust and psychological safety and encouraging cross-functional collaboration.

- Building strong relationships involves leading by example, fostering a supportive culture and organizing team-building activities.

"Innovation that matters happens with people."

- *N. Chandrasekaran*

Chapter 9
Recognizing and Rewarding Achievement

Introduction:

In this chapter, we explore the importance of recognizing and rewarding achievement in effective management. We delve into strategies for acknowledging and appreciating employee contributions, implementing effective recognition programs and providing meaningful rewards and incentives. By mastering these practices, managers can boost employee morale, increase motivation and create a culture of appreciation and excellence.

Acknowledging and Appreciating Employee Contributions:

Acknowledging and appreciating employee contributions is essential for fostering a positive work environment and motivating employees. Here are key strategies for acknowledging and appreciating employee contributions:

1. *Timely and Specific Recognition*: Managers should provide timely and specific recognition for employees' achievements. Acknowledging their efforts immediately and being specific about what they did well reinforces positive behaviour and encourages continuous excellence.

2. *Public Recognition*: Publicly recognizing employees' achievements, whether through team meetings, newsletters or company-wide announcements, helps create a sense of pride and boosts morale. Sharing success stories and showcasing outstanding performance motivates not only the recognized individual but also inspires others to strive for excellence.

3. *Personalized Appreciation*: Managers should take the time to understand each employee's preferences for recognition and tailor their appreciation accordingly. Some employees may prefer public recognition, while others might appreciate a personal note or a one-on-one conversation. Personalized

appreciation shows genuine care and appreciation for individual contributions.

Implementing Effective Recognition Programs:

Effective recognition programs provide a structured approach to acknowledging and rewarding employee achievements. Here are strategies for implementing effective recognition programs:

1. *Clear Criteria and Guidelines*: Managers should establish clear criteria and guidelines for recognition programs. Clearly defined benchmarks and metrics ensure fairness and consistency in the recognition process.

2. *Peer-to-Peer Recognition*: Encouraging peer-to-peer recognition empowers employees to appreciate their colleagues' contributions. Managers can establish platforms or systems for employees to nominate and recognize their peers, fostering a culture of mutual appreciation and support.

3. *Ongoing and Regular Recognition*: Recognition should be an ongoing practice rather than a one-time event. Managers should create opportunities for regular recognition, such as monthly or quarterly rewards/awards to consistently celebrate employee achievements.

Providing Meaningful Rewards and Incentives:

Meaningful rewards and incentives play a crucial role in motivating employees and reinforcing desired behaviour. Here are strategies for providing meaningful rewards and incentives:

1. *Individualized Rewards*: Managers should consider the preferences and interests of individual employees when selecting rewards. Tailoring rewards to align with employees' personal motivations and aspirations enhances their value and impact.

2. *Non-Monetary Rewards*: Rewards do not always have to be monetary. Opportunities for growth and development, flexible work arrangements, additional responsibilities or public recognition can be equally meaningful and motivating.

3. *Performance-Based Incentives*: Managers can design performance-based incentives tied to specific goals or achievements. This encourages employees to strive for excellence and rewards exceptional performance with tangible benefits.

- Success Story: N. Chandrasekaran

N. Chandrasekaran, the chairman of Tata Sons, understands the importance of recognizing and rewarding achievements. Under his leadership, Tata Consultancy Services (TCS) became one of the world's largest IT services companies. Chandrasekaran's focus on acknowledging employee efforts and providing meaningful rewards has played a vital role in TCS's success.

Summary of Learnings:

- Acknowledging and appreciating employee contributions boosts morale and motivation.

- Effective recognition programs provide structure and consistency in acknowledging achievements.

- Meaningful rewards and incentives align with individual preferences and reinforce desired behaviour.

"We need to create an environment where people feel free,

where people are empowered to do their best work."

-   Satya Nadella

Chapter 10
Continuous Learning and Adaptability

Introduction:

In this chapter, we explore the significance of continuous learning and adaptability in effective management. We delve into strategies for embracing a growth mindset, encouraging a culture of learning and adapting to change uncertainty. By mastering these practices, managers can stay ahead in a dynamic business landscape, foster innovation and lead their teams through challenges.

Embracing a Growth Mindset:

A growth mindset is a belief that abilities and intelligence can be developed through dedication, effort and learning. Here are strategies for embracing a growth mindset:

1. *Encouraging a Learning Attitude*: Managers should foster an environment where mistakes are seen as opportunities for growth and failures are viewed as stepping stones to success. By promoting a learning attitude, managers inspire their team members to embrace challenges and continuously seek improvement.

2. *Emphasizing the Power of Effort*: Managers should communicate the idea that effort and perseverance are key to achieving success. By highlighting the importance of hard work and dedication, managers encourage their team members to overcome obstacles and continuously develop their skills.

3. *Providing Learning Opportunities*: Managers should provide learning opportunities through various resources such as workshops, training programs and online courses. Offering these opportunities allows employees to acquire new knowledge, expand their skill sets and adapt to changing demands.

Encouraging a Culture of Learning:

Creating a culture of learning enables teams to thrive in a rapidly changing world. Here are strategies for encouraging a culture of learning:

1. *Lead by Example*: Managers should demonstrate their commitment to learning by engaging in continuous learning themselves. By modeling a thirst for knowledge and displaying curiosity, managers inspire their team members to do the same.

2. *Promote Knowledge Sharing*: Managers should create platforms and opportunities for team members to share their expertise, insights and lessons learned. Encouraging knowledge-sharing builds a collaborative environment and fosters a culture of continuous learning.

3. *Recognize and Reward Learning*: Managers should recognize and reward team members who actively pursue learning and show a commitment to personal and professional growth. Celebrating achievements related to learning encourages others to follow suit.

Adapting to Change and Uncertainty:

In today's fast-paced business landscape, adaptability is crucial for success. Here are strategies for adapting to change and uncertainty:

1. *Stay Informed and Proactive*: Managers should stay updated on industry trends, market dynamics and emerging technologies. Being proactive in anticipating change allows managers to prepare their teams and guide them through transitions effectively.

2. *Foster Agility and Flexibility*: Managers should promote a culture of agility and flexibility, encouraging team members to embrace change and adapt their approaches as needed.

Providing resources, support and guidance during times of change builds resilience and promotes adaptability.

3. *Encourage Innovation and Experimentation*: Managers should create an environment where experimentation and innovation are encouraged. By empowering team members to take calculated risks, managers foster a culture of adaptability and encourage creative problem-solving.

Success Story: Satya Nadella

Satya Nadella, the CEO of Microsoft, emphasizes the significance of continuous learning and adaptability in the digital age. Under his leadership, Microsoft transitioned from a software-focused company to a cloud-based services provider. Nadella's commitment to learning and innovation has driven Microsoft's growth and transformation.

Summary of Learnings:

- Embracing a growth mindset encourages continuous learning and development.

- Encouraging a culture of learning promotes innovation and resilience within the team.

- Adaptability is vital for navigating change and uncertainty in the business landscape.

Chapter 11
Conclusion

In this book, we have explored the key aspects of what **Great Managers** do differently. From the foundations of great management to empowering and developing employees, from effective communication to building trust and creating a positive work culture, we have covered a wide range of essential skills and practices. Throughout these chapters, we have drawn on the experiences of Great Industry Leaders to provide relevant examples and insights.

The central theme that emerges from this exploration is the importance of people-centred leadership. Great managers understand that their success lies in the success of their team members. They prioritize effective communication, active listening and building strong relationships. They lead by example, inspire others and empower their employees to reach their full potential. They recognize and reward achievements, fostering a culture of appreciation and motivation. They embrace continuous learning, adapt to change and promote a growth mindset.

The learnings from this book can be applied in various workplace settings, regardless of industry or organizational size. By implementing these practices, managers can create a positive work environment where employees feel valued, engaged and motivated. They can build strong teams that collaborate effectively, innovate and drive organizational success. These practices also contribute to employee satisfaction and retention, as individuals thrive in an environment that supports their growth and development.

As a manager, it is crucial to remember that great leadership is an ongoing journey. It requires self-reflection, learning and a commitment to personal and professional growth. By continuously honing these skills, managers can make a lasting impact on their teams and organizations.

In conclusion, the role of a great manager goes beyond task management and oversight. It is about building meaningful connections, empowering others, fostering collaboration and creating an environment where individuals can thrive. The journey towards becoming a great manager requires dedication, practice and a genuine concern for the well-being and success of your team. By applying the principles and strategies discussed in this book, you can become an exceptional manager who brings out the best in others and achieves extraordinary results.

Remember, you have the power to make a positive difference in the lives of your team members and the success of your organization. Embrace the principles of great management and embark on this rewarding journey of leadership.

Thank you for joining me on this exploration of **"What Great Managers Do Differently."** May your journey as a manager be filled with growth, success and fulfilment.

At the end let me say

Some of these strategies/successful practices you may have read or come across before.

But here's the deal: Your life won't change until your HABITS and PRACTICES change.

Merely reading or consuming success material doesn't change your life. I would encourage you to select your requisite strategy from this book and implement it in your daily life/organisation IMMEDIATELY.

Slowly but surely, you will begin to achieve things you never thought would have been possible...

If you liked this book, do consider leaving a review on Amazon. It only takes a few minutes but would help me tremendously.

I recommend you also read my other publications, titled

1. "Build a High-Performance Culture"

2. "High-Productivity Practices – From Successful Leaders – A Road to Success"

which are available on www.amazon.com / www.hroptimum.com

For other reading materials on HR management, please visit my blog page: https://hroptimum.com/blog

Your suggestions and comments would be most welcome. You may kindly do so at: coach.drravindran@gmail.com

Thank you so much!

www.ingramcontent.com/pod-product-compliance
Lightning Source LLC
Chambersburg PA
CBHW070359230526
45471CB00006B/2648